# Caring for the Dying

# with the Help of Your Catholic Faith

## Elizabeth Scalia

### Lorene Hanley Duquin
SERIES EDITOR

Our Sunday Visitor Publishing Division
Our Sunday Visitor, Inc.
Huntington, Indiana 46750

*Nihil Obstat:* Rev. Michael Heintz
*Censor Librorum*
*Imprimatur:* ✠ John M. D'Arcy
Bishop of Fort Wayne-South Bend
September 6, 2007

The Scripture citations used in this work are taken from the *Second Catholic Edition of
the Revised Standard Version of the Bible* (RSV), copyright 1965, 1966, 2006, by the
Division of Christian Education of the National Council of the Churches of Christ in
the United States of America. Used by permission. All rights reserved.

*Catechism* excerpts are from the English translation of the *Catechism of the Catholic
Church, Second Edition*, for use in the United States of America, copyright © 1994 and
1997, United States Catholic Conference — Libreria Editrice Vaticana. Used by
permission. All rights reserved.

Every reasonable effort has been made to determine copyright holders of excerpted
materials and to secure permissions as needed. If any copyrighted materials have
been inadvertently used in this work without proper credit being given in one form
or another, please notify Our Sunday Visitor in writing so that future printings
of this work may be corrected accordingly.

Our Sunday Visitor Publishing Division
Our Sunday Visitor, Inc.
200 Noll Plaza
Huntington, IN 46750

ISBN: 978-1-59276-239-2 (Inventory No.T290)
LCCN: 2007938183

Cover design by Amanda Miller
Cover photo: Shutterstock
Interior design by Sherri L. Hoffman

PRINTED IN THE UNITED STATES OF AMERICA

*For*
*Sal, Dennis, and Otto*
*Dear brothers gone too soon*

# Contents

# Facing the Unthinkable

After nearly a year of watching my brother grow progressively weaker from the effects of a serious illness, my family found things rather suddenly, dramatically, spiraling downward. A gregarious and loving family-minded person, my brother had over the past months been too weak to attend the birthdays and graduations he normally would never have missed, and lately we siblings and our parents had been spending more and more time at his house, telling ourselves we were merely keeping him company as he went through a rough patch.

But one morning, the telephone rang at an unforgivably early hour, and on the other end I heard my father, suddenly sounding very old and uncharacteristically afraid.

"Your mother went over to your brother's early this morning; she couldn't sleep. I'm afraid this time he is not going to make it . . ." his voice trailed off.

We talked for a few moments more, reassuring each other that things might still improve. In my mind I was thinking, "Yes, he is dying, my brother is dying." But those words were as yet unutterable to me, and I was in no hurry to bring them forth. I couldn't say something to my father that was at once becoming so obvious, and so breath-stealing. It felt like walls caving in.

I hung up from Dad and called another still-sleeping brother, who lived near him, and relayed the conversation. "He sounds scared, and I don't like him being alone. Why don't you go over and have breakfast with him?" I suggested. "We'll be there in a little while."

Thus we began a journey of the heart and the spirit that carried us through moments of sublimity and sorrow, from high good humor to holy and healing silence. It was a journey none of us wanted to walk, but one we found to be filled with grace and unexpected blessings.

## How This Book Can Help

The experience of caring for a loved one who is dying brings forth in us gifts and strengths that we otherwise would never believe we possessed. It taps into storehouses of patience and generosity that may have lain inside us for years, unused, like forgotten inventory in a warehouse that is rediscovered at exactly the right time, and for just the right customer. It is alternately wearying and uplifting, sometimes boring, and sometimes so trying that you wish you could simply run away.

No two people will experience it in the same way, with the same feelings. But for many, even those who do not think of themselves as particularly "religious," faith eventually enters in to the picture, sometimes in unexpected ways and in expressions that we do not always think of as "holy" — in anger, in fear, in desperate pleading — as well as in companionship and consolation, and ultimately, in mystery. The experiences of one person who is living through this ordeal will not — cannot — be exactly replicated by another's, because so much about each individual person is unique, and personal dynamics, faith, and even supporting players (who help out here and there) will contribute to the singularity of each experience.

> God had one son on earth without sin, but never one without suffering.
> — St. Augustine, 354-430

The purpose of this little volume is one of support and affirmation in the language and understanding of the Catholic faith. Its chapters are arranged in Way Stations — not unlike viewing stops on a long journey. Whether you are yourself facing the prospect of helping a loved one through his or her last days, or you are simply looking to share in the heavy burden of such a caretaker, it is hoped you will find meaningful and useful information and opportunities for reflection and insight along the way. You are embarking on a road difficult to travel, but one that can lead to spots of surprising beauty, and even, finally — unexpectedly — peace.

# A New Road, but You Are Not Lost

## A Time of Upheaval and Transitioning

There comes a point where doctors' appointments or short-term hospital-izations are no longer "sometimes things" but the in-and-out daily reali-ties of your life, a fact that is at once frightening and wearying. By the time you hear words like "nothing more can be done," or "consider long-term hospice," you may be feeling almost too exhausted to take the recom-mended next step: to find a visiting nurses' pro-gram to keep track of medicines, blood pressure, and various tests for monitoring. Usually, hospitals or clinics can help make those arrangements. They can help to get you started on that often-tricky path, one that some people find especially difficult, as it involves the inclusion of strangers not only into your grief and fear, but into your very own house. That startling intimacy can seem intrusive, and you may find yourself in a jumbled confusion of feelings:

> Jesus is the God whom we can approach without pride and before whom we can humble ourselves without despair.
> — BLAISE PASCAL, 1623-1662
> ~❦~

+ Fear that things have progressed this far.
+ Relief that someone with medical knowl-edge is on hand.
+ Anger that your life should have become this needful and vulnerable.

## Anticipatory Grief

This is a time of what is referred to as "anticipatory grief." This is very nor-mal, as you begin to anticipate how you may react to and cope with what can feel like an impending catastrophe. You might feel:

+ Numb
+ Angry
+ Tearful

- ✦ Helpless
- ✦ Anxious
- ✦ Absentminded
- ✦ Unable to pray

None of these feelings are wrong or unusual. "Anticipatory grief" affects us on every level — the physical, the mental, and the spiritual — particularly as you begin to move from the surface-denial that has kept

## Telling Children That Someone They Know Is Dying

How much a child comprehends about the concepts of death and dying depends upon both their age and maturity, and their religious instruction. Experts advise that when you talk to children about the impending death of a friend or family member, avoid the use of euphemisms — phrases like "going away" or "going to sleep." Using such phrases may cause a child to wonder if he or she did something wrong that made the person sick or drove them "away"; referring to death as being "asleep" has frightened more than one child into being afraid to go to bed at night! Uncomplicated language, using concrete ideas, will help children to better grasp what is going on around them. Very small children understand feelings and can respond to your simple declarations:

- ✧ Someone we love is very ill and we are sad.
- ✧ We wish things were different.
- ✧ This is a part of life.
- ✧ Even though we are sad, we are together, and that is good.

It's important to answer children's questions honestly and clearly, and to realize that no answer will ever fully satisfy them. As the journey you are on unfolds, they will be back with more questions, probably at surprising times. It's okay that you cannot answer those questions perfectly. No one can. Keep things simple and honest, even when discussing concepts of faith, and remember that it's perfectly all right to say to a child, "Well, I don't really know the answer to that." Children are not uncomfortable with the concept of mystery, and if you let them "have their heads," so to speak, they'll explore all sorts of ideas about what this part of life means. There can be real healing and consolation in such ruminations, and most importantly, you and the children have had time to talk together, and to wonder together. Together is good.

you afloat. "Well, today was a good day, perhaps tomorrow will be better" is about to give way to "We'll have to change our ideas of what constitutes a good day."

A new phase of this journey is unfolding, and friends and family who have been shielded from this process are now being filled in. All of this anticipates the day you will have to make the most difficult phone calls, giving the news of your loved one's passing. Indeed, you might begin to almost feel like you are in "rehearsal" for the coming "real" event. Just as an overture contains bits and snippets of an opera's more fully-explored themes, "anticipatory grief" is a foretaste of what you may feel later. It is a time to become acclimated. If you feel overwhelmed, you might take these steps:

+ Go for a walk.
+ Begin a journal in which you can safely express your feelings.
+ Consider joining a support group.
+ Confide in a friend or family member you trust.
+ Keep to what is familiar and simple, even in your prayer — *especially* in prayer.

## Feeling a Loss of Personal Control

Often up to this point, family and friends of the dying have not been thinking much about their own spiritual well-being. The opening of your home to hospital beds and IV stands (and all they represent) can precipitate a dizzying sense that things are now spinning completely out of one's control, and it can cause a desperate crying out, "God, please!"

But the prayer too often ceases, unable to find a focus. Without guidance, this prayer may simply fade into hopelessness. This is where, for you and your dying loved one, your Catholic faith can bring substantial help and consolation.

> The feeling remains that God is on the journey, too.
> — St. Teresa of Ávila, 1515-1582

## New Ways to Pray

Remember that any idea expressed to God can be prayer, no matter how simple. In fact, the things we say to God when we are unguarded and working "outside the lines" can often be our purest and most powerful prayers. They are the sorts of prayers that cannot help but end with an exclamation point, and often they are prayers not simply asking for help, but rather, demanding it.

Older Catholics might remember when such prayers were called "ejac- ulations." The word has fallen into disuse, but the image of prayer being forced from us (like water spurting from a pressured fountain-spout) is very apt. Our most desperate pleas can burst forth from us, unbidden, to bring some relief, some small sense of controlling something, and even a bit of companionship and peace. You might find yourself saying things like:

+ *Lord, have mercy!*
+ *Angels and saints, be with me!*
+ *Mother of God, pray for us!*
+ *I believe, Lord, help my unbelief!*

## Kinship with Jesus and Mary
Lean on your Catholic faith by remembering biblical and traditional scenes you have known all your life. Suddenly, they will speak to you in new and personal ways.

+ Watching a new, unknown person — someone who is not *you* — bathe your loved one may bring you a feeling of kinship with the Blessed Virgin Mary, who watched as a stranger, Veronica, wiped her Son's face.
+ For your loved one, that same experience might bring to mind the moment when a woman bathed Christ's feet and anointed them with oil.

With these feelings of understanding, of shared helplessness, you and your loved one may be able to explore matters of faith which have long gone un-addressed, and that might be helpful for both of you.

## Traditional Prayers *(see A Collection of Catholic Prayers, p. 59)*
You can begin to talk to God with the simple prayers learned in childhood, the Hail Mary or the Lord's Prayer. These familiar prayers may be spring- boards for more intimate conversation with God, wherein both you and your loved one can begin to bring forth and take control of your feelings of anger, fear, pain, and isolation. Praying familiar prayers out loud at the bedside of your loved one can be a source of consolation for both of you.

## Come Back Fearlessly, Even If You Have Been Away

This time of anticipation and transition is a good time to seek out spiritual direction and a bad time to worry about "bothering" someone, or of having been "too long away" from the Church. Priests, deacons, or pastoral associates understand that for so many people, facing the loss of a loved one is a circumstance that brings them to the rectory door, even those who have been "gone from church" for a while. It is the surest bet in the world that you will not be the first person they have ever met who, while "not really into church," has sought some assistance or information from them. They understand it, and they want to help.

> Likewise the Spirit helps us in our weakness; for we do not know how to pray as we ought, but the Spirit himself intercedes for us with sighs too deep for words.
> — ROM. 8:26

Even if you are not involved with a local parish, the hospital chaplain or a Catholic retreat center can direct you to trained spiritual directors or parish-sponsored support groups, and these can be a means of helping you make it through some of the difficult stretches of road still before you.

## Prayer and Reflection

It is not always possible to pray perfectly, or even well; even then, our God gives us the means of communicating with Him, through groanings of the Spirit and through the sacraments. Groan and speak now to the Lord, trusting that your feelings — your anger, your tears, your anguish, and your fears — are wholly acceptable to God, who is Love, and who will hear you.

### QUESTIONS FOR REFLECTION

1. What was my first encounter with death? How did I understand it then? How different is this reality?
2. Is it normal to want to run and hide, even as I see people reaching out to me, to help?
3. How can I find God in the midst of all of these conflicting, scrambled feelings?

# The Quiet Riot

## Dealing with Others

When a family member is dying, you begin to see a few old faces — friends you have not seen in ages, cousins for whom "getting together" has been nearly impossible, people from the past with whom you may have severed relations due to misunderstandings.

Let them in, if you can, without resentment or suspicion. Try to give the benefit of a doubt to someone who has shown up "out of nowhere" and roused some ancient negative feelings. Sometimes old family business, old wounds, might color how we receive these folks. You may find yourself fuming inside: *Why are they here?* or *How nice of them to show up* now!

Actually, yes, it *is* nice of them. If someone is taking the time to make what we all know is a difficult visitation, do yourself a favor and allow yourself to appreciate it. None of us manages to get through our lives with the purest and noblest intentions; that is one of the reasons we have the helpful Sacrament of Reconciliation (or Confession). It is a means by which the Church helps us to reconcile ourselves to God and to the world around us.

> It is not the magnitude of our actions but the amount of love that is put into them that matters. At judgment, God will see only the love.
> — BLESSED TERESA OF CALCUTTA, 1910-1997
> ~❧♥❧~

## Speak the Unburdening Words

Right now, you might want to consider taking advantage of what that sacrament has to offer — the opportunity to unburden yourself of all of the feelings you have been holding close, feelings you dare not express to others but wish to speak out loud. The Sacrament of Reconciliation:

- ✦ Allows you to express yourself freely in objective company.
- ✦ Promises complete confidentiality. No priest is permitted to discuss what he has heard within the discourse of confession.

- ✦ Relieves fears, doubts, and guilty feelings.
- ✦ Bestows necessary graces to aid you in dealing with (and getting caught up in) those same anxieties once more.

Taking part in the Sacrament of Reconciliation brings you right smack-dab into the middle of the mystery of Christ's mercy. And when you have been shown mercy, it is much easier to show it to others. Somehow, that forbearance and kindness all comes back to you in the end. Sacramental grace also helps us stay aloft in those areas in which we routinely fall short.

As to those visitors who might cause some unrest, credit them with the best intentions until they show otherwise. Doing so will make your life a little easier.

## Speaking the "Other" Unburdening Words

As helpful as a dose of sacramental grace may be, there are times when you encounter a person who simply doesn't get it, or who may be what we could generously call "tact-challenged." While a soft answer may turn away wrath, that does not mean that rudeness, inappropriate questions and comments, or glaring insensitivities must be continually overlooked.

When my brother was being bathed or turned, we would sometimes wait in a gathering room and chat with family members of other patients with whom we had become friendly. One memorable evening, the discussion meandered into dealing with these "insensitive" types, and one woman forthrightly said, "Sometimes people are just shaken up to be around all this death and dying, and they say stupid things, and you have to just let that go. But I can't tell you how many times this week I've wished I had a big fish!"

> While you are proclaiming peace with your lips, be careful to have it even more fully in your heart.
> — St. Francis of Assisi, 1182-1226

"A big fish?" I asked. "What on earth for?"

She smiled. "To give some of these people one good thwack upside the head!"

I would not recommend the "thwacking fish" method of dealing with rudeness, but there are ways of addressing intrusive or nosy questions, plodding remarks, or rank stupidity. They're even more effective if you can manage an expression of incredulity while you respond:

- ✦ *Why in the world would you possibly ask that?*
- ✦ *That's really not something with which you need concern yourself.*

✦ *I think perhaps you meant to say that differently, or do I mistake your meaning?*

Everyone wants to be nice, but being nice doesn't mean that others have to know all of your business; people need only as much information as you care to share. You have a right to your boundaries.

Sometimes, even medical staff can be distracted by many duties and seem less sensitive to your situation than you expect. Remember that — as strange as it may seem — while caring for a dying loved one is a uniquely personal situation for you, to many medical professionals, the process of dying is almost routine. Thus, they can seem removed and cold, even when they don't mean to be.

> We are afflicted in every way, but not crushed.
> — 2 COR. 4:8
> ⚜

That doesn't mean that you can't gently remind hurried doctors, nurses, and others that the patient they are dealing with is not just a set of symptoms and a med chart, but a beloved human being who deserves their full attention and respect. Most medical personnel, caught up in rounds and responding to beepers, will, when reminded that the person in the bed is "someone's parent, someone's grandparent, someone's spouse, someone's sibling," pull back and realize when they've moved too far into an efficiency mode and try to correct that.

## When Everyone Wants to Help

"What can I do to help?" Have you ever said those words? Someone gives you some bad news, and you gasp and say, "Is there anything I can do?"

When you're asked that same question, don't be afraid to say "Yes." You may need someone to take a child to an appointment or check on the dog a few times a day. What you might think of as a burdensome chore may feel to a friend or family member like the only genuine help they can render. They are happy, even honored, to help out. Just use your best judgment when deciding whether or not to accept offers of assistance; sometimes, for whatever reason, you may want to decline. Either way, answer as gratefully as you can:

✦ *Thank you. To be honest, I have been unable to (water the plants, walk the dog, pick up the laundry), and if you are sure it wouldn't be too much trouble, you would really be helping me out.*

17

+ *Thank you, but your prayers mean so much to us. You could do nothing better!*
+ *Really, knowing how busy you are, your visits (or phone calls) are already so generous, and we are so thankful for them.*
+ *Thank you. I do appreciate your asking, but we seem to be handling things.*

Be prepared for food and baked goods to come your way. Visitors often come bearing baskets of fruit, cakes, and cookies. No, you cannot eat it all — that's what nurses are for! Thank your gifting friends graciously, even if it is the third cake you've received this week. Accept the overabundance of goodies for what they are: tokens of affection and esteem from people who feel a deep need to do something, even when they know there's little that can be done.

## Dealing with Yourself

Both in the world and in the Church, we are discouraged from extremism or narrowness of focus. In the world, narrowness precludes openness; in the Church, we find that taking a too-thin perspective can wrap us up in an excessive scrupulosity that pushes away both mercy and love. And yet . . . if ever there was a time when laser-like intense focus seems appropriate, caring for a dying person may be it.

> What saves a man is to take a step. Then another step.
> — C.S. Lewis, 1898-1963

Still, you cannot expect to function at your best if you don't allow yourself some respite, a little leeway in the new world full of "musts" and "shoulds" and schedules and responsibilities. Life requires that you give yourself elbow room and breathing space if you are to be at your most effective and alert. In other words, at a time when you are inclined to think only of someone else, it is essential that you think a little bit about yourself, too. You need to keep the body "walked and aired" and the mind refreshed, even though thinking up ways to do that can feel exhausting in itself. So do the things that have always been naturally enjoyable for you.

+ Get some light exercise, preferably in fresh air.
+ If weather or energy does not permit a short walk, a half-hour in a rocking chair can be a remarkably effective means of gently getting your blood moving, and the motion is itself comforting. If the air is only a little chilly, consider wrapping yourself up in a

comfortable blanket and rocking near a slightly opened window or, even better, on the front porch.

+ Breathe. Close your eyes, sit comfortably, and concentrate on breathing in and out. Your body will thank you.

+ Look out the window while you drink your coffee or tea, for some bird-and-people watching.

+ Play a song, album, or CD you have not heard in a long time.

+ If you are a crafty sort or a hobbyist, get out an old project or collection and allow yourself to concentrate on it a bit. You're not being self-indulgent, and you still won't have to finish it in those few minutes, but you will be amazed at how energizing you will find it to briefly focus on something that simply makes you happy.

+ Eat ice cream with a kid and appreciate the mess. Things can always be cleaned later.

It would be nice — indeed, it would be heroic — if in the midst of caring for your dying loved one, you could remember to send a birthday card to Aunt Sarah, or manage to find the time to attend the baseball game of a nephew. But really, it is perfectly okay to drop the many balls you have been juggling in order to stay focused on what is most important.

Be gentle with yourself; forgive yourself if you have forgotten a date or a promise made. God's job is forgiveness, and He does it enormously well. If He can forgive so much, can't you forgive yourself a little?

## Prayer and Reflection

When St. Bernadette Soubirous, the visionary of Lourdes, was repeatedly questioned by Church officials about her visions of Mary at Massabielle and the spring of healing waters that arose from that place, she would patiently respond, "My job is not to convince you, only to inform." For a peasant girl of that era to speak so forthrightly was considered a little scandalous, but Bernadette was not being fresh-mouthed. She was simply being clear. Lift up a quiet "attagirl" to Bernadette now, and perhaps ask her to be with you as you try to remain kind to others while being true to yourself and clear in your communication. It is all part of the "communion of saints," both in this world and the next.

## QUESTIONS FOR REFLECTION

1. Words mean things. What words are uppermost in your mind today?
2. Dropped balls can be picked up. What can you let go of right now?
3. How are you dealing with other people at this difficult time?

# The World As It Is

## Reality Bites Us

He was a first-class mystic, but Pope John Paul II also had a pragmatic streak. He would often caution his advisors and his audiences that, in considering any situation, you must remember one limitation: you must deal with the world as it is.

Death is a reality of life — the last reality on an earthly plane. Since it is the last reality, it is an easy one to push to the edges of your awareness and never think about until you have to. Now, you have to. As you face the death of someone you love, it is very natural to find yourself considering your own mortality, and wondering about things both practical and unknowable:

+ *What do I believe happens when we die?*
+ *Time moves so quickly; am I using it well?*
+ *Who will take care of my family, my pets, my friends, when I am gone?*
+ *Have I told everyone how much I love them?*
+ *Have I made my own preferences clear?*

That last question is a very dynamic one, and it is often the catalyst for enlightening discussion. Facing the death of someone we love gives way to serious talk about what dying means to people and what concerns

---

Death is the end of earthly life. Our lives are measured by time, in the course of which we change, grow old and, as with all living beings on earth, death seems like the normal end of life. That aspect of death lends urgency to our lives: remembering our mortality helps us realize that we have only a limited time in which to bring our lives to fulfillment.

— *CATECHISM OF THE CATHOLIC CHURCH*, 1007

---

they have. Unfortunately, in trying to be sensitive to others, we often mistakenly think we need to have such conversations out of earshot of the dying person. It can be a surprise when we realize that often the opposite is the case. Someone facing death and feeling isolated might like nothing better than to talk about what he or she is thinking and discovering. Family members "in the thick of it" may also very much want to share this process they are undergoing — the process of facing reality, of losing control, of saying goodbye.

## Keep the Lines of Communication Open

Try to be the open line that encourages people to talk. Let your loved one, your family, and your friends know that they can talk to you and that you want to know what they're thinking and feeling, no matter how mundane it may seem. Let your friends know that it's safe to talk to you about the process in which you are engaged, that they needn't pussy-foot around the subject to spare your feelings. Talking openly and fearlessly about death is one way to unshackle yourself from hesitancy and doubt.

Helping someone make his or her wishes plain is another way to feel more in control of all that is going on around you. Death is part of life, after all, and a most mysterious part. While the pain and sense of loss it brings is uncommon in our lives, it's certainly not uncommon in the world, where every day brings death and sadness to someone. It's not easy to endure, but if it were unendurable, the world would have stopped long ago. Instead, we continue. We live. We even thrive.

## What Happens After Death

Where someone is after death is certainly a topic for exhaustive discussion. It may well be one of the things you find yourself pondering with sympathetic friends and family, or with your loved one, or both.

What does the Church teach about death and life after death?

✦ *We are loved into being.*
✦ *Life is a gift.*
✦ *Life is sacred, and one who is alive should be allowed to live the life she or he has. Death is another stage in life, one into which we all will pass.*
✦ *Through death, we touch the Eternal.*
✦ *God is Eternal.*

## What Is Purgatory?

A place of purification — a sort of way-station for the soul, wherein our imperfections may be rendered perfect so that we might stand before God. In Dante Alighieri's *Divine Comedy*, we read that the souls in purgatory are happy even though they suffer (by being outside of God's company), because they know that they are promised heaven.

Will I go to heaven? Will my loved one?

In his book *The Divine Milieu*, the Jesuit priest and writer Pierre Teilhard de Chardin prays, "You have told me, O God, to believe in hell. But you have forbidden me to think, with any certainty, of any man as damned."

That last question is the hardest one, and no one can answer it except Christ and the person standing before Him. Some people are so holy we have no doubt they will quickly be smiling at us from a heavenly plane, but sometimes — if we are honest — we cannot be so certain. As Christians, we can take comfort in the fact that Jesus is merciful, and God is love, two facts that hold great promise. And it is good to remember this: no one knows what happens between a soul and Christ in those infinitesimal moments between the last vestige of this life and entry to the next. But perhaps in those moments, even if we have spent our lives not seeking out His mercy, we find it, despite ourselves.

## Body and Soul

At this point, you may be beginning — perhaps for the first time in your life — to consider matters of the spirit and of eternity. How funny, then, that in these almost palpably supernatural moments, we must focus so intently upon the body, on the natural and physical.

Human life is sacred because from its beginning it involves the creative action of God and it remains for ever in a special relationship with the Creator, who is its sole end. God alone is the Lord of life from its beginning until its end: no one can under any circumstance claim for himself the right directly to destroy an innocent human being.

— *Catechism of the Catholic Church,* 2258

The Church has always strongly acknowledged the inseparable link between body and soul, and how the treatment of our body directly affects the condition of our soul. The medical care of your loved one may now be primarily centered on:

✦ Pain management
✦ Nutrition and hydration
✦ Palliative care (the total care of patients who are not responsive to curative treatment)

Some people are surprised to discover that the *Catechism of the Catholic Church* would address such seemingly benign and obvious medical issues as these. The *Catechism* is a very comprehensive (and comprehensible) document that can provide much clarification on sometimes confusing subjects. Looking into the above issues, we read, in part:

2278. Discontinuing medical procedures that are burdensome, dangerous, extraordinary, or disproportionate to the expected outcome can be legitimate; it is the refusal of "over-zealous" treatment. Here one does not will to cause death; one's inability to impede it is merely accepted. The decisions should be made by the patient if he is competent and able or, if not, by those legally entitled to act for the patient, whose reasonable will and legitimate interests must always be respected.

2279. Even if death is thought imminent, the ordinary care owed to a sick person cannot be legitimately interrupted. The use of painkillers to alleviate the sufferings of the dying, even at the risk of shortening their days, can be morally in conformity with human dignity if death is not willed as either an end or a means, but only foreseen and tolerated as inevitable. Palliative care is a special form of disinterested charity. As such it should be encouraged.

Of course, beyond the management of pain and nutrition, you may find yourself facing other questions:

## Is Organ Donation Allowed?

While addressing an international convention of transplant scientists, Pope John Paul II said, "... one way of nurturing a genuine culture of life 'is by the donation of organs, performed in an ethically acceptable manner, with a view to offering a chance of health and even of life itself to the sick who sometimes have no other hope.'"

## Where Does the Church Stand on Artificial Respiration and Feeding Tubes?

Pope Pius XII wrote in his letter *The Prolongation of Life* that in "hopeless" cases, including cases of permanent unconsciousness, treatments such as resuscitation and respirators "go beyond the ordinary means to which one is bound." Thus there is no obligation "to give the doctor permission to use them" (p. 397).

In a 1992 draft text of a statement by the Sacred Congregation for the Doctrine of the Faith, we read:

> The condition of the person, especially those who are dying, e.g. persons in the final stages of Alzheimer's, cancer or renal failure, or in the state commonly called a persistent vegetative state must be considered in decisions to discontinue or forego life sustaining treatment.

The subsequent text, released in July 1992, defined more clearly the "dying person" as one "who has no reasonable hope of recovery." It cautioned that "rational reflection on the meaning of human life in all its dimensions is indispensable for formulating a moral judgment of the use of technology to maintain life."

Pope John Paul II made his last years a sort of living testament to the value of a single human life, no matter what his or her condition. As he lay dying in late March of 2005, his care briefly included a nasal/gastric feeding tube, meant "to improve his calorific intake and promote an efficient recovery of his strength . . ." When he, his attendants, and his physician determined that there would be no further recovery, the feeding tube was removed and simple intravenous hydration continued until the pontiff breathed his last. Nothing was done to either hurry or impede death, which simply came naturally.

## Does the Church Allow Catholics to Have a "Do Not Resuscitate" Order?

Overall, the position of the Church on these end-of-life issues may be said to be very sensible. Cardinal Sean O'Malley of the Archdiocese of Boston gave these very clear instructions to his flock:

Allowing to die is very different from taking life. The underlying illness is the cause of death when futile or excessively burdensome treatment is withdrawn or withheld. Catholic teaching calls us to recognize the limits of medical technology. DNR orders and decisions to forgo artificial nutrition and hydration in some situations of terminal illness can be morally acceptable options.

## Is a Health Care Proxy Preferable to a Living Will?

Living Wills concern themselves primarily with questions pertaining to the use of technology to prolong life — they are usually asking a "yes or no" question about whether a person wishes machinery to be used to save or prolong a life. As such, they tend to leave a great deal up to the medical community, rather than one's family and friends. Some bishops feel this is insufficient, as it does not provide for individual circumstances. According to the National Catholic Bioethics Center (NCBC), an Advance Directive with a Durable Power of Attorney or a Health Care Proxy is preferable. Either will allow a patient to designate authority to make important health care decisions on his or her behalf. This interested and concerned party can, in turn — due to personal and sympathetic knowledge — express the patient's desires to physicians and caregivers. In such a way, a patient's sensibilities are not disregarded or treated expediently.

Hospitals and hospice have forms for Health Care Proxy available. The Eternal Word Television Network also has printable forms for Advance Directives and Health Care Proxies that can be downloaded at: http://www.ewtn.com/expert/answers/Directive.pdf and http://www.ewtn.com/expert/answers/Proxy.pdf.

This all sounds like a lot to think about: the details are daunting, even overwhelming, and the conversations are too awkward to open. They need not be. If you aren't up to it, or if you simply need a bit of help, don't hesitate to ask a nurse or hospital chaplain to assist you in broaching such subjects with your loved one. They're used to it — you won't be the first person who has ever asked for their assistance in such a way.

And the chances are your loved one has been wondering how to bring it all up, too.

## Prayer and Reflection

While we may fondly wish to live out our days in simplicity, this process shows us just how complicated every phase of life can be; details are important. In the days leading up to Passover, Jesus instructed a few of His apostles to go to a certain man, to see about a particular room, and to make arrangements for the Passover. No detail was overlooked, but Jesus did not see to them Himself. Perhaps knowing, as He did, that this meal was to be His last on earth, made those details seem overwhelming.

*Remind me now, Lord, that You, too, have been concerned and preoccupied by details, and by enough foreknowledge to anticipate sad days. You taught us that the most difficult part of any task is simply consenting to do it. I consent, Lord, to the details. Please be my guide and comfort through them.*

## QUESTIONS FOR REFLECTION

1. How does care of the body, in sickness and in health, affect the soul?
2. Life "as it is" can be complicated. How can communication help?
3. Is an Advance Directive something I should suggest to my loved one? Is it something I should do for myself?

# The View from Down Here

D own here" is where we are when we're feeling a little crushed and defeated, and "down here" looks like a vulnerable and scary place to be. But, difficult as it may seem, you will not feel this way forever.

## When Doing It Yourself Is No Longer Feasible

For many, the moment hospice is first mentioned is the most "down there" moment of the journey, the nadir, the rock-bottom. "Hospice" means that the one you love is — barring a miracle — not expected to survive. It means that prayers change and hopes do, too. Whether hospice is at home or away, it is recognition that reality has become too large to be self-contained, and that other doors must be opened and other hands grasped:

+ Visiting nurses
+ Home heath assessors and social workers
+ In-home hospice care
+ Care at a hospice facility

The whole concept of hospice is unfamiliar to some people. Generally, a patient enters hospice treatment when it has been determined that nothing further can be done. At this point, the patient is given palliative care: making him or her comfortable, managing pain, and providing whatever nutrition and companionable consolation might still be possible. It is pure "end of life" care.

It is not unusual for a family to cringe at the idea of hospice, because it is a concept all about finality — something that can be difficult to face.

For my own family, consenting to hospice was a bitter decision with which not everyone agreed. My mother was inconsolable at the idea that there was nothing more we ourselves could do to maintain my brother's comfort and well-being. For some, remembrance of promises made to my brother (that we would all take care of him to the end) overrode practicality, to the point that we began to make ourselves ill trying to keep our word. Our hearts wanted to do the difficult work of seeing to his constant and many needs, but our bodies and our life circumstances forced us to face up to the reality of what we could and could not do.

I remember telling my brother that we older ones were making a decision to place him in hospice care, in an excellent facility with brightly colored walls and opportunities for us to take him to the outdoor pavilion. "Your bed has become your world," I said. "With the help of this place, we'll be able to actually give you a little more freedom and mobility."

"Freedom and mobility," he mused. "I'm game." But that game face was frightened. He was disconcerted by the idea that his care was leaving the trustworthy hands of family and moving into the hands of strangers, and he wasn't alone in that. Mere hours after his admittance, however, he was more comfortable than he had been in weeks, and we all found our best hopes realized.

> Somebody should tell us, right at the start of our lives, that we are dying. Then we might live life to the limit, every minute of every day.
> — POPE PAUL VI, 1897-1978

## Hospice Brings Time

What hospice brings, besides a consoling, helping hand, is the gift of time, re-appreciated and re-learned. Suddenly "time" takes on fuller meaning; it is not simply about medicine schedules and appointments. It becomes, once again, about shared moments.

When my brother went into hospice, my exhausted family was not sure what it would mean beyond extra help. We found that it meant the bettering of time — the improvement of time spent together — a re-acquaintance with the concept of "quality time." Time had become frightening before, because it seemed so fleeting. Suddenly, time became precious, warm, and enlarging. Suddenly, there was time — time to make the best of whatever moments we had left together, and that perception became a huge positive to a reality that had become all too negative.

## Time Brings Grace and Mystery

Along with the gift of time, hospice also provides some breathing room. In-home or out, hospice gives you a chance to feel human again — to get a haircut or even a manicure without extreme anxiety or guilt, to attend a family gathering for a few hours and realize that yes, things are changing, but things are also in many other ways staying the same. Much of what you already know and love will remain, even after all of this strange newness has passed.

To illustrate to yourself what it means for things to remain, even when your whole world seems about to become unrecognizable, you might take a look at a Catholic calendar of feast days and holy days. In doing so, you will not only get a chance to visit with some wonderful saints, but you will get a sense of things "changing, yet remaining the same." Our calendar mixes festal occasions with commemorations of church dedications, important moments from the life of Jesus and the Blessed Virgin, and more.

Within the context of every different memorial or feast, the Mass is unchanging, Christ's presence is unchanging — therefore, what is different is always anchored in what is familiar, in the comfort of sameness. It seems paradoxical that your life, while traveling along a path of unstoppable change, will still — unbelievably — be recognizable to you in the end, but you may count on it.

## The Lives and Deaths of the Saints

Take some time to think about the men and women who have gone before us and to realize that these good people — some famous, some obscure — all lived on this earth and then died. They all took the same journey you see before you in one way or another, and you can talk to them about it. We declare in the Apostles' Creed that we believe in the Communion of Saints. Those who have led the way in faith are still near,

> Therefore, since we are surrounded by so great a cloud of witnesses, let us also lay aside every weight, and sin which clings so closely, and let us run with perseverance the race that is set before us.
> — HEB. 12:1

and in their shared humanity, there is much to which we can relate.

While what you are currently going through feels unique, and in many ways is unique and singular because it involves you, it helps to reflect on how very ordinary is the work of living and dying.

Sometimes, there is wisdom in just opening your arms to the mystery of it all, and letting God do the rest.

## Prayer and Reflection

In some ways, the surrender to the need for hospice care is not unlike Christ's surrender at Gethsemane, where Jesus prayed one last time for deliverance, for a cup to pass Him by, before finally accepting all that would come next. Many simply ascribe His acquiescence to His divinity. *Easy to trust what comes next*, we think, *when you are God, after all.* But Jesus was also fully human, and He knew fear and uncertainty. It is because He was both God and man that we can turn to Him now, join Him in that dark but fragrant garden, and weep and ask for reprieve. When we rise and surrender, we do it in the company of the Lord who knows precisely what it costs us, this trust. Gethsemane is no Eden, but we are never alone there, either.

> Then Job answered the LORD:
> "I know that you
> can do all things,
> and that no purpose of
> yours can be thwarted."
> — JOB 42:1-2

---

## QUESTIONS FOR REFLECTION

Change is the stuff of our lives, nothing is static; everything is in a constant state of flux, as the ticking of a clock. Change is, in fact, one thing we may always count on.

1. What changes in your life are surprising to you? Is what has remained constant also a surprise?
2. In the midst of all of this, do you feel like you are losing yourself?
3. God is "ever ancient, ever new." In this process of swift evolution, what thoughts and feelings are "old" and "new" within you?

# Take Control Where You Can

Around the time my brother was brought into hospice, he would occasionally say something like, "When I die, I want to be cremated, and my ashes thrown off a mountain in Hawaii." Because we were unprepared to have such discussions, we would joke, "You know we hate to fly. Will Staten Island do?"

He wasn't serious about cremation or Hawaii, and we weren't serious about ignoring his wishes, but it took a while for us to be able to talk openly about his impending death, and what he wanted the last "gathering" for his sake to be like.

We did learn how to do it, though, and it turned out to be good for him and for us that we did. Helping someone you love to plan a funeral and see to legal matters, like wills and title transfers, achieves several things:

✦ It lets everyone — the dying person and caregivers alike — feel productive instead of helpless.

✦ Important decisions will not be left until the awful day comes, when your brain may feel like it has "stopped working."

✦ This planning, selecting, and discussing may be the last thing you really get to "do" together. And in a way, you are helping each other.

✦ Lots of spontaneous communication takes place in all this planning. Expressions of love, fear, and loss do not get held back. It is a very good and ultimately comforting thing.

## Making Arrangements

When it looked like my brother would not be with us much longer, two of us were selected to look into "making arrangements," and two others took on the task of sorting out business matters. "Let's do this now, while we have our heads about us, when we are not running on emotion," we said. My brother was in this way able to help and to make his preferences known in every area. For all of us, it was a chance to feel in control of some things, which is heartening when so much is being taken out of your hands.

Business and estate matters more or less took care of themselves. Where he could, my brother dispersed his possessions to friends and family as he desired, and we took care of the rest. Knowledgeable family members prevented us from needing an attorney, but in most cases it is probably smart to consult with one, particularly if there is a large estate involved, or if there are ownership and possession issues within the family.

It's generally a positive thing for a person who is dying to make a legal will, thus insuring that his or her wishes for the dispersal of properties will be followed. Your loved one might be reluctant to do so, either because he fears the expense or she does not wish to "insult" anyone by being "too exacting" or by accidentally "leaving someone out." With your help, though, that last concern can be avoided.

The cost to draw up a will varies depending on where you live, the size of the will, and how much time was needed by a lawyer to prepare it. It's unusual for a will to be exorbitant in price, and the fees may well "pay for themselves" if they help to keep a family running smoothly.

## Funeral Planning

The more time-consuming matter for us involved helping my brother with funeral and burial considerations. This might seem to be a very difficult series of conversations to have, but my brother initiated it by mentioning how much he liked a particular hymn, and how he hoped it would be played at his funeral. Rather than joking with him as we had previously, this time we respectfully listened to him, and we asked if he would like to talk about his preferences in music, readings, and the rest.

---

I wanted a perfect ending. Now I've learned, the hard way, that some poems don't rhyme, and some stories don't have a clear beginning, middle, and end. Life is about not knowing, having to change, taking the moment and making the best of it, without knowing what's going to happen next. Delicious Ambiguity.

— GILDA RADNER, 1946-1989

---

Suddenly what had seemed appallingly difficult to broach became very natural. Our attention to him, and our willingness to hear him, and to seek out ways to achieve his desires, was an affirmation of just how valuable he was to us. It gave him dignity. And though our hearts were very heavy as we went about our tasks, we also felt it was a privilege to do this with him.

Having ascertained from our *Catechism* that cremation was a permissible option for a Catholic, we asked my brother if this was still his wish. It was not. My brother wanted, for his own sake and for ours, a funeral Mass, formally referred to as a Mass of Christian Burial. We were glad we asked!

> The Church permits cremation, provided that it does not demonstrate a denial of faith in the resurrection of the body.
>
> — *Catechism of the Catholic Church*, 2301

When people choose cremation, the Church prefers that the cremation be performed after a Mass of Christian Burial, but if that is not possible, or if a body is not available for other reasons, a Memorial Mass may be performed. In ritual and prayer, both Masses are very similar.

## Practical Considerations

Pay attention to what your loved one is saying to you. You can demonstrate that you are listening by asking pointed questions:

- ✦ *What do you like about that song/hymn/reading/poem?*
- ✦ *Does it have special meaning for you?*
- ✦ *Would you like me to make sure it is read/played/sung for you?*

Once it has been established that it is okay to talk about the funeral, wake, and burial, you may be surprised to find that your loved one may be very specific — even insistent — about some things. He or she may wish to talk about:

**Burial clothes.** One of our family members wanted to be buried in a team sweatshirt. We didn't much like it, but that's what she wanted, and she got it.

**Sentimental items.** Does your loved one want special items in the casket, such as a First Communion pin, a picture, a "lucky coin," a football, a favorite pair of shoes?

**Flowers**. Does your loved one want lots of flowers at the wake and funeral? Or would he or she prefer that mourners make donations to a particular charity or research fund?

**Pallbearers, readers, and others**. Although a dying person may not want to ask them directly, he or she may wish for you to ask certain friends and family members to act as pall bearers, readers, musicians or vocalists.

**Eulogies**. Some parishes permit a friend of family member to offer a short eulogy immediately after Communion. Other parishes do not permit eulogies in the church and ask that they be done at the wake, during the committal at the graveside, or during the funeral brunch. If your loved one wants a eulogy, it is a good idea to find out what is permitted at your parish.

**Hymns and music**. Most parishes supply families with a list of hymns and songs deemed acceptable for funerals, and it is a good idea to work from that list, since it is music the parish musicians can play well. Some parishes will try to accommodate requests outside of the norm, provided they are respectful and appropriate to the occasion.

> For everything there is a season, and a time for every matter under heaven.
>
> — Eccl. 3:1

**Readings**. Again, most parishes can provide a helpful selection of readings. Encourage your loved one to choose the readings that most speak to him or her.

**Interment**. It is no longer required that Catholics be buried in a Catholic cemetery. The priest can bless the gravesite if a community cemetery is chosen. If cremation has been selected, does your loved one wish his or her ashes to be entombed in a cemetery vault designed for that purpose, or would he or she prefer to have the remains buried in the grave of another family member?

**Graveside prayers**. The committal service may be performed by a priest or deacon.

I have attended funerals where the deceased was played into and out of church to the solemn strains of a single bagpipe. If your loved one wishes for something out-of-the-ordinary, it is best to check with your parish to see what they permit.

Making funeral arrangements is not easy, but once all of these matters were settled and in place, it made it much easier for the family to simply be together. We had the comfort of knowing that my brother had a voice in nearly every aspect of his funeral and liturgy.

## Prayer and Reflection

When Jesus visited the sisters, Mary and Martha, Mary sat at his feet and took instruction. Martha bustled about attending to details. Right now, your life might feel a little bit like Martha's life, with all the worry and movement. It might feel a little like Mary's life, too, inspiring you to sit down and simply contemplate where you are and what you believe. There is prayer in silence; it is often in silence that we can hear life. Sit quietly now, and hear the silence and the prayer of your own heart, before getting up to hurry some more.

## QUESTIONS FOR REFLECTION

1. What things are really and truly in your control today?
2. Does it feel all right to you to be thinking along such practical lines while in the midst of such emotional upheaval? Why or why not?
3. Can you remember a funeral you attended that struck you as genuinely consoling and healing? What made it so for you?

# The Hidden Garden Along the Way

Scripture talks to us of gardens — Eden, Gethsemane, the garden of the lovers who inhabit the Song of Songs, a garden of delight and sweetness. There is yet another garden in your future, one that may be reached through sheer attentiveness. It is an autumnal garden, one in which the last scented roses linger surprisingly on the bush; a few sweet grapes tempt from a vine, even as the warming sun fades and the air begins to sting.

My brother brought us into this garden when he relaxed into what he called his "job of dying." We found it in the surprising jokes that came from his exhausted lips, in a wry tease, a roll of the eyes. In that garden, a tiny bit of himself was still showing, like a green leaf peeking through the branches; it reassured us that no matter how different he looked or seemed, he was still the man he had always been.

These moments came and went, and each time they did, we held onto them as we would a fragile flower at season's end, pressing the petals between the pages of our memory. Seek out the garden of autumn; be attentive. Don't let the petals drop unobserved. You will treasure them.

## Angels in Our Midst

The hospice staff made my family and my brother feel as though we were truly in the presence of angels. The nurses and orderlies who filled his days became his newest and most intimate friends. They knew death,

---

The angel of such radiant beauty knelt before the angel of the dying and the sick. Then, like a tribute from a novice to a hierophant, she held two Roses out to her . . . the loveliest of the garden.

— FRANZ LISZT, 1811-1886

❧

---

## Prayer to Your Guardian Angel

"I will now declare the whole truth to you and I will not conceal anything from you. I have said, 'It is good to guard the secret of a king, but gloriously to reveal the works of God.' And so, when you and your daughter-in-law Sarah prayed, I brought a reminder of your prayer before the Holy One; and when you buried the dead, I was likewise present with you. [. . .] I am Raphael, one of the seven holy angels who present the prayers of the saints and enter into the presence of the glory of the Lord. But he said to them, "Do not be afraid; you will be safe. But praise God forever." —TOBIT 12: 11-12, 15, 17

*O Guardian Angel, whose name is known only to the Creator, St. Jerome taught "how great the dignity of the soul, since each one has from his birth an angel commissioned to guard it." I pray you remain in my awareness, that I be mindful of the great gift of your company and protection. Trusting in the words of the Archangel Raphael, who said to Tobit and his wife, "the way is safe," I ask your patience as I lean a while on you, seeking your strength and your support. Keep me always mindful of the goodness of God and the bounties placed before me which are sometimes difficult to see with my human eyes. Stay with me, friend and protector, and accept my grateful thanks. Amen.*

they were not afraid of it, and they brought enormous generosity to everything they did. They bucked us up, brought us a sense of normalcy, and gave us the feeling that nothing we were about to encounter was insurmountable. Like the Archangel Raphael in the Book of Tobit, they walked a difficult road with us, gladly and unconditionally, all the way to the end.

> Then he [Tobit] said to [Tobias], "Go with this man [Raphael]; God who dwells in heaven will prosper your way, and may his angel attend you." — TOBIT 5:16

We Catholics are not always as acquainted with our guardian angels as we used to be, but that doesn't mean they are no longer there.

> For he will give his angels charge of you to guard you in all your ways.

On their hands they will bear you up, lest you dash your foot against a stone. — Ps. 91:11-12

You can talk to your guardian angel, no matter what your age. Acknowledge your unmindfulness and ask for company through these difficult days. You will be answered. You have never been as alone as you have believed, and maybe today is the day to make the acquaintance of your heretofore-constant companion, your angel. We have human company, both for better or worse, and we have our angels, who can help us rise to our better selves. Really, you are not alone. Between the last moments in the garden and the renewed relationship with your angel, you may be better able to deal with all that is about to transpire.

> We cannot pass our guardian angel's bounds, resigned or sullen, he will hear our sighs.
> — St. Augustine, 354-430

## The "Job of Dying"

Keeping aware of angels and a mindset of "the garden" was a big help once we discovered just what my brother meant when he joked about his "job of dying." Over a period of weeks, as my brother transitioned from this life to the next, we learned that the process of dying fully engages the body, the mind, the emotions, and the spirit, in the following ways:

### The Physical

As death approaches, a dying person can exhibit some or all of the following behaviors, apart from those symptoms specific to his or her illness:

- Excessive sleepiness as energy wanes.
- Decreased appetite as metabolism slows.
- Difficulty in swallowing.
- Sleeping with eyes partially open (to conserve energy).
- Changes in responsiveness and alertness.
- Restless movement which includes kicking or picking at sheets and blankets.
- Urinary and bowel changes.

Often, a person who is dying will be appalled by the physical changes taking place inside them and by their lack of control. They will need reassurances that none of this is making them at all "unlovable."

### The Mental/Emotional

A person who is dying is often fearful; they can also experience moments of joyfulness and periods of worry. Be loving and understanding as you are made privy to his or her thoughts and emotions, which may include:

+ Concerns about those they leave behind.
+ Agitation over unsettled business or personal affairs.
+ Regrets for what has been left unsaid or undone.
+ Expressions of needfulness and vulnerability.
+ Misplaced anger directed at anyone, including you, but really meant for another or even for oneself.

These feelings are very normal, and while witnessing them can sometimes be wearying for a caregiver, you can often soothe the teeming thoughts and emotions with simple acts:

+ Reassure him or her that everything possible has been done for others, and that these unsettled feelings are normal.
+ Hold your loved one's hand.
+ Offer to read from a favorite book or play some favorite music.
+ Give your loved one the opening to say whatever he or she feels.

### The Spiritual

Persons who are dying often seem to be "half-in-and-half-out" of heaven, seeing and hearing things we cannot see and hear. They may express interest (or opposition) to speaking with a member of the clergy. They may ask you to pray for them, or even with them. As supernatural instincts seem to become heightened, you may observe the dying person:

+ Reacting and responding to stimuli others do not sense.
+ Claiming that he or she can see deceased relatives.
+ Having conversations with persons from his or her past.
+ Want to pray or to talk about religious and spiritual matters.

When you encounter this, don't argue, tell them they are imagining things (you don't really know that), or discount what they are telling you. Rather, simply be present with them, and open to what is happening. You might ask, with love:

+ *"Who is it you are talking to?"*

✦ *"What are you seeing?"*

✦ *"How does that make you feel?"*

Allow the dying person to share this with you. As a Catholic, you might discuss the Communion of Saints, what St. Paul called "so great a cloud of witnesses" (Heb.12), and which supports the concept of those who have gone before us surrounding us, as in a mist or cloud, and still accessible to us via prayer. We find it explained this way in the *Catechism of the Catholic Church:*

> In the communion of saints, "a perennial link of charity exists between the faithful who have already reached their heavenly home, those who are expiating their sins in purgatory and those who are still pilgrims on earth. Between them there is, too, an abundant exchange of all good things" (*CCC*, 1475).

## Praying With Someone Who Is Dying

Sometimes my brother really wanted to pray but he did not have much energy, so he would ask us to pray with him. While extemporaneous prayer is always good, sometimes weary hearts and minds cannot find the words. While we know that the Holy Spirit intercedes for us with "groaning too deep for words," (Rom. 8:26) it is sometimes helpful to fall back on familiar prayers and devotions:

✦ The Lord's Prayer
✦ The Rosary
✦ The Kyrie
✦ The Glory Be
✦ The Divine Praises
✦ Readings from the Psalms and the Gospel
✦ The Prayer to St. Michael the Archangel

If your loved one has not already been anointed (or if he or she was anointed previous to this new stage of illness), they might feel inclined to be anointed and prayed over now. If your loved one is at home, call your local parish and ask for a priest to come. If your loved one is in the hospital or in a hospice facility, ask the hospital chaplain to make arrangements for the Sacrament of the Sick.

## Prayer and Reflection

The Way of the Cross is an ancient devotion in which Catholics walk the *Via Dolorosa* (Way of Sorrows), recalling the Passion of Jesus Christ. For many of us who have cared for our loved ones as they found their completion, the road seems joyless and the burden too heavy. On a bad day, we think of Christ falling beneath the weight of His cross; we see His mother watching Him with agony written in her face, and we identify with all of it. Watching the one we love weaken a little more each day, it almost seems like we are watching the Passion of the Christ play out before our eyes.

## The Sacrament of the Sick

When my brother was doing poorly but was still at home with visiting nurse care, some in the family resisted the idea of having him anointed in the Sacrament of the Sick. For them, the idea spoke too much of what used to be called Extreme Unction, or Last Rites. It seemed too much like losing hope and giving up. And, too, the idea of a priest coming into the home was unusual and a little uncomfortable: *What will it be like? Will the house have to be spotless? Who has energy to clean when our focus is so completely on our loved one? Will the priest stay for supper? But none of us is even eating these days; we have no appetite!*

Once the family understood that the Sacrament of the Sick was not the passing of an immediate death sentence, but an anointing that carried with it absolution and healing grace (of both the physical and spiritual varieties), a simple phone call was all it took. An appointment was made; a priest my brother knew slightly came to us, sat with us, talked and prayed with us, and briefly, with my brother alone.

Then, we gathered together and watched as the priest anointed and prayed over him, asking for his healing and absolving him of his sins. My brother smiled, sighed in contentment, and thanked the priest, who was soon on his way.

"That was really nice," someone said. "I am so glad we asked Father to come."

My brother nodded in agreement. "I am, too," he said. "Why did we wait?"

42

> Let nothing disturb you, let nothing frighten you. All things are passing. God never changes. Patient endurance attains all things. Who God possesses, they want for nothing, and God alone is sufficient.
> — St. Teresa of Ávila, 1515-1582

Not only are we watching it, we are living it. Swabbing parched lips, we remember Christ on the cross — "I thirst" — and suddenly, the small hydrating sponge we touch to our loved one's lips is the very one used to console Jesus, who is before us. At that moment the mystery to which we have tried to open ourselves becomes overwhelming. But in that moment, we can also realize that there is nothing we are experiencing that is foreign either to God-who-is-Man, or to His mother. You can pray without words, merely visualizing an image from the *Via Dolorosa*, and they are near.

## QUESTIONS FOR REFLECTION

1. In the midst of all of this pain, has there been some beauty?
2. Is it possible to have love without pain?
3. How does the process of dying reflect the process of living?

# The Long Tunnel

Some people say the process of dying involves the appearance of a long tunnel through which one passes, moving toward light. Just as those who report back from a "near death experience" say they felt "pushed along" through a tunnel, you may feel like you are being "pushed along" by circumstances, and unable to halt the forward motion — a prisoner of sheer momentum. You would be right. As the journey's end nears, there seems to be no further chances to hit the brakes or to pull back a bit.

> I have been able to follow my death step by and now my life goes gently to its end.
> — POPE JOHN XXIII, 1881-1963
> ❧❦❧

This is a scary feeling. A new skier would never attempt an advanced trail, and yet here you are moving through this experience at a breathtaking pace. Everything seems out of your control. This might be a good time to make an assessment of what you can control. You can control being wholly present to a person who is dying. That doesn't seem like very much, but it is everything.

## Together with Our Lady

When Mary, the mother of Jesus, was told that her Son had been arrested, her world also began to spin out of control. In truth, you are very much Mary's companion right now, just as she is yours. What you are living through, she has survived:

✦ Just as your access to your loved one is decreasing as their need for sleep increases, Mary's access to her Son was closed off.

✦ Like you, Mary had to stand by and watch helplessly while her loved one took on the "job of dying."

✦ Like you, Mary had to watch the one she loved let go of her to take His leave.

44

> When Jesus saw her weeping, and the Jews who came with her also weeping, he was deeply moved in spirit and troubled; and he said, "Where have you laid him?" They said to him, "Lord, come and see." Jesus wept. So the Jews said, "See how he loved him!"
>
> — JN. 11:33-36

- ✦ Mary, too, had to let go, and to trust that she would see Him again.
- ✦ As you lean on family and friends, remember that Mary had John and Mary Magdalene beside her for support.
- ✦ After Jesus' death, Mary had to live and eat and worship with an imperfect "family," some of whom had let her — and her Son — down. It is not really a unique experience, as families go.

Being "wholly present" may not feel like you are doing very much. It may seem like a pitiful amount of "control" for an adult to have over any person or event. But as Mary taught us, being "present" to another person has power. It is saying, "I will be a witness to your whole life and death, so that all you are and have been will remain in me, when you have gone. And I will help you say goodbye."

Being wholly present to a dying person is a great responsibility, one that requires all the control of which you are capable.

## Saying Goodbye

One night I sat by my sleeping brother's bed, reading a book. He opened his eyes and in a frail voice announced that he was going.

"Where are you going?" I asked.

"I am going to Florida," he said.

Leaning over to kiss his brow, I said, "Well, you've got your ticket, and we've all said goodbye. If you really have to go, you can leave. We'll see you again!"

"Thank you," he murmured, ever polite.

My brother did not "go" that night, or even that week, but things had progressed to the point where all of our family members had the opportunity to say goodbye to him, and to whisper loving words — and he had the chance to whisper them back.

It is said that there are five things people need to say before they die:

*"Forgive me."*
*"I forgive you."*
*"Thank you."*
*"I love you."*
*"Goodbye for now; we will be together again."*

> "Lord, now let your servant depart in peace, according to your word."
> — Lk. 2:29

You can help someone you love to say those words by saying them first, and by encouraging other family members to say them, where appropriate. This can happen very naturally, as visitors come and go, over days and even weeks. Encourage it. Let the words and the declarations happen.

No, there is not very much within your control right now, but you can help things along by simply being present, and everyone — most especially your loved one — will be more grateful than they perhaps even realize for your doing it.

## Prayer and Reflection

When Jesus stepped onto His final path, He, too, must have felt incapable of stepping off of it, of slowing down events. He, too, might have yearned for options that were no longer there; so once again, we find ourselves, in these bleak moments, face-to-face with the One who understands. Christ is here. Like the sisters of Lazarus, who lived in Bethany, you can run to Him. Greet Him now and tell Him all that is in your heart. It is very safe to do this. And, as He wept with the two women, if you weep, He will weep with you.

> *Lord, moved with compassion for the keen grief You saw in Martha and Mary and the others who mourned Lazarus, You wept, even though You knew what they did not know. Look with compassion on me now. I do not know what You know, and cannot see what You can see. I know only that I am weary and tired in spirit and body. Please remain with me. Come and see my days and nights. I entrust them to You now.*

1. What in life has prepared you for this process of letting go?
2. How scary is it to feel out of options?
3. When in your life have you felt someone be wholly "present" to you?

# Destination

### The Final Vigil

It is said that the last prayer uttered by St. Francis, on his deathbed, was Ps. 141, which includes this passage:

*But my eyes are toward you, O Lord God; in you I seek refuge.*

If you are attempting a final vigil, the Psalter is a very useful resource. The psalms are perfect and poetic reflections of the human experience, and they are also powerful expressions of prayer.

Consider using Ps. 130:

*Out of the depths I cry to you, O Lord!*
*Lord, hear my voice!*
*Let your ears be attentive*
*to the voice of my supplications!*
*If you, O Lord, should mark iniquities,*
*Lord, who could stand?*
*But there is forgiveness with you,*
*that you may be feared.*

> [The sun's] rising is from the end of the heavens,
> and its circuit to the end of them;
> and there is nothing hidden from its heat.
>
> — Ps. 19
>
> ~*~

Ps. 23, "The Lord is my shepherd," is useful, as is Ps. 51, the *Miserere*:

*Have mercy on me, O God,*
*according to your merciful love;*
*According to your abundant mercy blot out my transgressions.*
*Wash me thoroughly from my iniquity*
*and cleanse me from my sin!*

Also useful is this canticle from Is. 38:

*I said, in the noontide of my days*
  *I must depart;*
*I am consigned to the gates of Sheol*
  *for the rest of my years.*

*I said, I shall not see the* LORD
  *in the land of the living,*
*I shall look upon man no more*
  *among the inhabitants of the world.*
*My dwelling is plucked up and removed from me*
  *like a shepherd's tent;*
*like a weaver I have rolled up my life;*
  *he cuts me off from the loom;*
*from day to night you bring me to an end.*
  *I cry for help until morning;*
*like a lion he breaks all my bones;*
  *from day to night you bring me to an end.*
*Like a swallow or a crane I clamor,*
*I moan like a dove.*
*My eyes are weary with looking upward.*
*O* LORD, *I am oppressed; be my security!*
*But what can I say? For he has spoken to me,*
  *and he himself has done it.*
*All my sleep has fled*
  *because of the bitterness of my soul. [ . . .]*
*but you have held back my life*
  *from the pit of destruction,*
*For you have cast all my sins behind your back.*

## Destination

When my brother finally succumbed to his illness, it was immobilizing. With all of the anticipation, the reality of his passing still short-circuited our wiring. I recall suddenly being unable to successfully dial a phone. You might experience something like this: an unexpected sense of shock may well accompany this very *expected* leave-taking. Here is your destination, at least in practical terms — the end of the tunnel, the beginning of a few days unlike any other. If you have been keeping a bedside vigil, sharing prayers with family members, you may have had a final sense of your loved one as he or she departed, or not.

> God planned, in the fullness of time, to restore all things in Christ.
>
> — LENTEN ANTIPHON TO MORNING PRAYER

49

It seems to happen with curious frequency that dying persons make their exit when family members are near but not gathered 'round. You may leave the room for just a few minutes to refresh yourself and return to find that they have "slipped away." Sometimes you may not immediately recognize that death has come, thinking at first only that the person seems to be resting more comfortably. This is not unusual.

When my brother died, my mother was extremely distraught because she felt she had failed him by not being "there" with him when he passed. Hospice nurses, who are daily witnesses to the dynamics of this process, were quick to reassure her that most deaths occur when family members have briefly stepped away. Truly, while not "being there" when a loved one passes may cause you to feel sad, there is no reason to feel guilty.

Here are some practical things you should know:

✦ If death has occurred at home, take time to say goodbye. When you are ready, you will call either your hospice coordinator or funeral director. You will likely have contact numbers to go to,

## Prayers after Death

Here are some prayers that can be said after the death of a loved one:

*God of power and mercy, You have made death itself the gateway to eternal life. Look with love on our dying brother/sister, and make him/her one with Your Son in His suffering and death that, sealed with the blood of Christ, he/she may come before You free from sin. Amen.*

*Lord Jesus, our Redeemer, You willingly gave Yourself up to death, so that all people might be saved and pass from death into a new life. Listen to our prayers; look with love on Your people who mourn and pray for their dead brother/sister. Lord Jesus, You alone are holy and compassionate; forgive our brother/sister his/her sins. By dying, You opened the gates of life for those who believe in You; do not let Your brother/sister be parted from You, but by Your glorious power, give him/her light, joy, and peace in heaven, where You live for ever and ever. Amen.*

particularly if you have had any sort of visiting nurse or home health care assistance.

+ If death has occurred in a hospital or hospice facility, you will be given time alone with your loved one before the funeral director is called. You do not have to pray at this time, but you may do so if you wish.

+ The funeral home will contact your parish with the vital information and schedule the funeral details.

## The Next Few Days

When my brother passed on, even though it was anticipated, we all found ourselves enormously undone. Having all of the wake and funeral arrangements settled and in place made it much easier for the family to simply come

## Children, Wakes, and Funerals

While children who have attended Sunday Mass with their parents may not find much that is remarkable about a funeral Mass (aside from the sadness all around), wakes can be very tricky for young children and teenagers. There is no absolute and correct answer to the question of whether a child should attend a wake. That question depends entirely upon the emotional maturity of the child, and the ability of his or her parents and other family members to help them process what they are experiencing for the first time. Some families do not bring their young people to wakes. Some do, but with the understanding that the child or teenager will hang on the periphery of the waking room, or even in the lobby of the funeral home. Other families determine that their children (and the family) have the collective resources to address any questions or emotions that come up.

If children are to participate in a wake, be prepared to explain things to them. Because they are curious, they may ask questions, and it's all right if you don't know the answers. But some family members should be ready to remind young people of the following things we as Catholics believe:

✧ *It will be all right. We are all together and our lives will go on.*

✧ *Our loved one has seen Christ.*

✧ *We will see our loved one again.*

together to console one another and be together. And we had the added comfort of knowing that my brother had had a hand in choosing just about everything that would occur over the course of the next few days.

If you have not already prepared a liturgy or decided on a funeral Mass or a prayer service, you will now. If you have had the opportunity to put all of that in place, you can catch your breath, gather together with family and friends, and think about what is immediately ahead, which is the wake.

Here are some wake customs and traditions you may want to consider:

+ Displaying photos of the deceased at every age and stage of life.
+ If permissible, playing background music that he or she particularly loved.
+ Group prayer, as in the rosary or a responsorial psalmody, during the wake.
+ Readings of a favorite poem or personal letter that you want to share.
+ A brief prayer service by a priest, deacon, or pastoral associate.

## The Funeral

Liturgical prayer has long played a part in the comings and goings of humanity. Five thousand years ago, our Hebrew ancestors chanted *Kaddish*, the prayer for mourners, which greatly praises and exalts God. Even today, we look for a way to reconcile life and death, and to commend it all to God. We still do it because it helps. It heals.

> All shall be well, and all shall be well, and all manner of things shall be well.
> — BLESSED JULIAN OF NORWICH, C.1342-1420

Because we had involved my brother in the funeral plans, the liturgy became a truly healing experience. My family entered the church exhausted, emotionally fragile, bent over, feeling beaten. But as the familiar readings, favorite hymns, and formal prayers of the liturgy progressed, I looked at my family and noticed that we were sitting straighter, listening attentively, nodding, kneeling, praying. We were allowing all that was familiar and "normal" to wash over us, to bring us a sense of otherness, of something other and greater than ourselves, and of great promise. It helped us with all of these other, newer feelings.

There was victory in the liturgy, and a conquering. Here was the Church Triumphant: "O death, where is your victory; O death, where is

> Not till the fire is dying in the grate,
> Look we for any kinship with the stars.
> Oh, wisdom never comes when it is gold,
> And the great price we paid for it full worth:
> We have it only when we are half earth.
> Little avails that coinage to the old!
>
> — GOLDA MEIR, 1898-1978

your sting?" (1 Cor. 15:55) And here was my brother, with us again, one more time.

## Passing Through

At funeral's end, the casket makes its way through the church, toward the doors and the waiting transport. It has always seemed to me eloquently expressive of our short time here on earth.

> . . . a thousand years in your sight are but as yesterday when it is past, or as a watch in the night . . . our years come to an end like a sigh. The years of our life are threescore and ten, or even by reason of strength, fourscore; yet their span is but toil and trouble; they are soon gone, and we fly away.　　— Ps. 90:4, 9-10

We are all only passing through, from an illusion of time into timelessness, returning to the Eternal from which we sprang. Let us pass without fear, trusting that our lives, infinitesimal in the sight of the Ages Unto Ages, may pass through into glory, and trusting in the mercy of God.

## Prayer and Reflection

*Like a swallow or a crane I clamor,*
*I moan like a dove.*
*My eyes are weary with looking upward.*
*O Lord, I am oppressed; be my security!*

　　　　　　　　　　　　　　— Is. 38:14

*Lord, I take You at Your Word and trust You, as You have promised mercy. Have mercy on those I love, those who are now living and those who have passed. Our lives truly are in Your hands. Help me to remember that today is only a day, a blink to Eternity, and all of its difficulties and its pleasures will come to an end. You, however, are always with me, ages unto ages.*

## QUESTIONS FOR REFLECTION

1. How does it feel when you reach a destination?
2. Once we have reached a destination, do we stay there forever?
3. Where do you want to go from here?

# After

After a funeral or prayer service, after a shared meal, after the clutched hands and hugs, after the thank-you notes, but before the full return to practical living, it is time to rest, even if only for a little while.

## Sorting Out the Feelings

Over the next few days and weeks, you will experience myriad emotions — and that is perfectly normal. What will also be normal, but unsettling to some, will be the unexpectedly mixed feelings you may experience in the weeks and months immediately after the funeral. Aside from the expected feelings of sadness, anger and loneliness, you may discover surprising senses of:

✦ Gratitude that your loved one is no longer suffering.
✦ Relief that a very hard job has come to an end.
✦ Guilt for daring to feel either gratitude or relief when your loved one has died.

Do not burden yourself. These are the utterly normal feelings that too often cause people to beat themselves up psychologically. The simple fact is that in the midst of your intense sadness, it is no contradiction to be both deeply grieved over your loss and somewhat relieved that a terrible ordeal has ended for both you and the one you lost. An interior conversation occurs — usually in otherwise quiet moments — that seems to run in an unending loop of tension and release. It goes something like this:

(Tense) "I feel so bad. I can't believe he's gone —"
(Sigh) "Thank you, God, that he is no longer suffering."
(Tense) "Although I wish we had had more time —"
(Sigh) "But honestly, I was so exhausted I don't know if I could have gone on."
(Tense) "What a horrible person to think such a thought! Am I a horrible person? I feel so bad. I can't believe he's gone —"
(Sigh) "Thank you, God, that he is no longer suffering."

Don't succumb to that tape running through your mind or give in to feelings of guilt. No one wants you to ruminate in this fashion, and it is neither a fair judgment of yourself nor a healthy obsession. God doesn't want it. Your family and friends don't want it. Your loved one wouldn't want it. If you find you cannot shut down that tape without help, don't hesitate to seek out assistance in group therapies or work with a bereavement counselor. Nothing you have just been through has been easy. And grief is — to one extent — just more hard work.

## Catching a Holy Breath

You may not be able to "rest" as well or as easily as some others can; some people simply cannot leave work undone and feel at ease. You may not wish to, in fact. Some of us prefer busy-ness to being alone with our thoughts. It's good to remember that holy rest does not require becoming a layabout; it simply is an invitation to "rest awhile in Me."

When Jesus died, His followers and His mother retired to an upper room — partially to hide, but partially to rest and recover from a trying ordeal, to catch their breath before going on.

Breath is the province of the Holy Spirit, who came to them in the upper room, their resting place. The resurrected Christ said, "Receive the Holy Spirit," as He breathed on them. He also promised, "And I will ask the Father, and he will give you another Counselor, to be with you for ever" (Jn. 14:16).

> O Holy Spirit, descend plentifully into my heart. Enlighten the dark corners of this neglected dwelling and scatter there Thy cheerful beams.
> — St. Augustine, 354-430

A counselor or an advocate is one who is on your side. Your lawyer may be considered your advocate, into whose hands you might place all your legal concerns. Just so, you can place the concerns of your heart and spirit into the keeping of the Third Person of the Trinity, and know that you can rest in confidence, before moving on.

### Veni, Creator Spiritus

*Come, Holy Spirit, Creator blest,*
*And in our souls take up your rest;*
*Come with your grace and heavenly aid*
*To fill the hearts which you have made.*

*O Comforter, to you we cry,*
*O heavenly gift of God Most High,*
*O fount of life and fire of love,*
*And sweet anointing from above.*

## Bereavement Groups and Diocesan/Parish Help

Perhaps the Holy Spirit may lead you to seek out others who are recently bereaved and dealing with loss. Most parishes host small bereavement or support groups, or if they do not, they can direct you to a neighboring parish that does. To seek out such a group commits you to nothing, obligates you in no way. You will not be asked to run something (you have just "run" too many things). You will not be asked to be instantly and wholly recovered from your grief, or even to say a word, if you'd rather not. You will simply be welcomed. Here you might, like Mary and the apostles — who rested together before rising to begin their new and lifelong work — take a breath with others who, too, are sighing for a little while.

## Rising

*O God,*
*when the women came*
*to anoint the body*
*of Your crucified Son*
*they wondered who would*
*roll away the stone from His crypt.*

*I ask You now*
*to roll away the heaviness of spirit*
*that has come from the work of caretaking*
*and the sadness of leave-taking.*

*I know that in Your time*
*we will understand all mysteries*
*and be reunited in love and in your glory.*

*As I stop to take a Holy Breath,*
*I ask You to be with me,*
*O Father*
*O Son*

*O Holy Spirit*
*to remain in me and with me*
*as I rise, once more, to go on*
*to move forward.*
*to live in Your peace,*
*and to do Your will. Amen.*

# A Collection of Catholic Prayers

### The Lord's Prayer (The Our Father)

*Our Father, Who art in heaven,*
*Hallowed be Thy Name.*
*Thy Kingdom come.*
*Thy Will be done, on earth as it is in Heaven.*
*Give us this day our daily bread.*
*And forgive us our trespasses,*
*as we forgive those who trespass against us.*
*And lead us not into temptation,*
*but deliver us from evil. Amen.*

### The Hail Mary

*Hail Mary, Full of Grace,*
*The Lord is with thee.*
*Blessed art thou among women,*
*and blessed is the fruit*
*of thy womb, Jesus.*
*Holy Mary, Mother of God,*
*pray for us sinners now,*
*and at the hour of death. Amen.*

### The Glory Be

*Glory be to the Father,*
*and to the Son,*
*and to the Holy Spirit.*
*As it was in the beginning,*
*is now, and ever shall be,*
*world without end. Amen.*

## The Apostles' Creed

*I believe in God, the Father Almighty, Creator of Heaven and earth; and in Jesus Christ, His only Son Our Lord, Who was conceived by the Holy Spirit, born of the Virgin Mary, suffered under Pontius Pilate, was crucified, died, and was buried. He descended into Hell; the third day He rose again from the dead; He ascended into Heaven, and sitteth at the right hand of God, the Father almighty; from thence He shall come to judge the living and the dead. I believe in the Holy Spirit, the holy Catholic Church, the communion of saints, the forgiveness of sins, the resurrection of the body and life everlasting. Amen.*

## The Kyrie

*Kyrie eleison; Christe eleison; Kyrie eleison.*
*Lord, have mercy; Christ, have mercy; Lord, have mercy.*

## The Act of Contrition

*O my God,*
*I am heartily sorry for*
*having offended Thee,*
*and I detest all my sins,*
*because I dread the loss of heaven,*
*and the pains of hell;*
*but most of all because*
*they offend Thee, my God,*
*Who are all good and*
*deserving of all my love.*
*I firmly resolve, with the help of Thy grace,*
*to confess my sins,*
*to do penance, and to amend my life. Amen.*

## Prayer for Healing

*Lord, You invite all who are burdened to come to You. Allow Your healing hand to heal me. Touch my soul with Your compassion for others. Touch my heart with Your courage and infinite love for all. Touch my mind with Your wisdom, that my mouth may always proclaim Your praise. Teach me to reach out to You in my need, and help me to lead others to You by my example. Most loving Heart of Jesus, bring me health in body and spirit, that I may serve You with all my strength. Touch gently this life which You have created, now and forever. Amen.*

## Prayer to St. Michael the Archangel

*St. Michael the Archangel,*
*defend us in battle.*
*Be our defense against the wickedness and snares of the Devil.*
*May God rebuke him, we humbly pray,*
*and do thou,*
*O Prince of the heavenly hosts,*
*by the power of God,*
*thrust into hell Satan,*
*and all the evil spirits,*
*who prowl about the world*
*seeking the ruin of souls. Amen.*

## The Divine Praises

*Blessed be God.*
*Blessed be His Holy Name.*
*Blessed be Jesus Christ, true God and true man.*
*Blessed be the name of Jesus.*
*Blessed be His Most Sacred Heart.*
*Blessed be His Most Precious Blood.*
*Blessed be Jesus in the Most Holy Sacrament of the Altar.*
*Blessed be the Holy Spirit, the Paraclete.*
*Blessed be the great Mother of God, Mary most holy.*
*Blessed be her holy and Immaculate Conception.*
*Blessed be her glorious Assumption.*
*Blessed be the name of Mary, Virgin and Mother.*
*Blessed be Saint Joseph, her most chaste spouse.*
*Blessed be God in His angels and in His Saints.*
*May the heart of Jesus, in the Most Blessed Sacrament, be praised, adored, and loved with grateful affection, at every moment, in all the tabernacles of the world, even to the end of time. Amen.*

# Resources

**Books:**

*Catechism of the Catholic Church*. Image; New edition, 1995

Bill Dodds, *Your Grieving Child: Answers to Questions about Death and Dying*. Our Sunday Visitor, 2001

Michael Dubruiel, *The How-To Book of the Mass*. Our Sunday Visitor, 2006

Lorene Hanley Duquin, *Fighting Cancer with the Help of your Catholic Faith*. Our Sunday Visitor, 2005

————, *Grieving with the Help of Your Catholic Faith*. Our Sunday Visitor, 2006

Mary Lou Rosien, *Managing Stress with the Help of Your Catholic Faith*. Our Sunday Visitor, 2006

Glenn Spencer, *Blessed Are Those Who Mourn*. Our Sunday Visitor, 1999

**Online Hospice and Caregiver Information:**

http://www.hospice.com

http://www.cancerthroughacarerseyes.jkwh.com/

http://www.caringinfo.org/i4a/pages

**Online Resources for Talking with Children about Death:**

http://www.kidsaid.com/dougypage.html

http://www.kidshealth.org/parent/emotions/feelings/death.html

Online Vatican Resource for the Address of John Paul II to the 18th International Congress of the Transplantation Society:

http://www.vatican.va/holy_father/john_paul_ii/speeches/2000/jul-sep/documents/hf_jp-ii_spe_20000829_transplants_en.html

## Online Resources for Living Wills, Feeding Tubes, and Artificial Respiration:

http://www.rcab.org/Healthcare/Notes/EthicalDecisionsatEOL.htm
http://answers.google.com/answers/threadview?id=197616
http://www.ncbcenter.org/eol.asp
http://www.ewtn.com/expert/answers/end_of_life_decisions.htm
http://www.cnn.com/2005/WORLD/europe/03/31/pope1/

## Online Prayer Resources:

http://www.ewtn.com/Devotionals/prayers/index.htm
http://www.scborromeo.org/prayers.htm
http://www.2heartsnetwork.org/deceased.htm